D0206764

Prairie Schooner Book Prize in Poetry · EDITOR : Hilda Raz

Famous

Kathleen Flenniken

University of Nebraska Press

Lincoln and London

"Map of the Marriage Bed" is
reprinted from the *Prairie Schooner*
by permission of the University of
Nebraska Press. Copyright 2004 by
the University of Nebraska Press.

"Reading Hamilton's Biography of
Robert Lowell" contains an excerpt
from "Epilogue" from *Collected Poems*
by Robert Lowell. Copyright © 2003
by Harriet Lowell and Sheridan
Lowell. Reprinted by permission of
Farrar, Straus and Giroux, LLC.

LIBRARY OF CONGRESS
CATALOGING-IN-PUBLICATION DATA
Flenniken, Kathleen.
  Famous / Kathleen Flenniken.
    p.   cm.   — (Prairie schooner
  book prize in poetry)
  ISBN-13: 978-0-8032-6924-8
  (pbk.: alk. paper)
  ISBN-10: 0-8032-6924-2
  (pbk.: alk. paper)
  I. Title. II. Series.
    PS3606.L47F36 2006   811'.6—dc22
    2005030816

Set in Monotype Dante by A. Shahan.
Designed by A. Shahan.

For Steve

Contents

III Fame

Acknowledgments

My thanks to the editors of the following magazines in which many of these poems first appeared:

Atlanta Review: "The League of Minor Characters," "Sea Monster"
Cider Press Review: "One Night, an abridged biography of
   Shirley Jackson," "Sarah Chang plays violin," "Shampoo"
Clackamas Literary Review: "Elisabeth Reads Poetry,"
   "Prayer Animals"
Crab Creek Review: "If We Could Live Here," "The Nuns' Remains,"
   "What I Saw"
Cumberland Poetry Review: "Anaïs Nin on the Sales Table,"
   "How to Read this Story to your Children"
Green Mountains Review: "It's Not You, It's Me,"
   "The Sound of a Train"
Hayden's Ferry Review: "Conversation with a Sensualist"
Heliotrope (vol. 6, Fall 2005): "The Beauty of the Curve"
The Iowa Review: "To Ease My Mind," "The Physiology of Joy,"
   "Sotto Voce," "My father invented the calendar"
Literal Latte: "LOST COAT, PLS CALL,"
Mid-American Review: "Natural History"
Natural Bridge: "Passing for Mormon"
The Nebraska Review: "Fireball," "Preservation"
Northwest Review: "The International House of Pancakes,"
   "Lessons in Trigonometry"
Poet Lore: "The Minor Celebrities"
Poetry (December 2003): "Woman Reading"
Prairie Schooner: "Map of the Marriage Bed"
The Seattle Review: "Words drift down on Virgil Suarez"
South Carolina Review (Spring 2004): "Calling Up Ghosts"
The Southern Poetry Review: "Gil's Story" (in a slightly different
   version), "Graphology"
The Southern Review: "What I Learn Weeding"
Two Rivers Review: "Dust"

"Graphology" was reprinted in *Farm Pulp*.

"LOST COAT, PLS CALL" was reprinted in *Seattle Woman*.

"Lessons in Trigonometry" and "Woman Reading" were reprinted in *Art Access*.

"Sea Monster" and "The Sound of a Train" appeared in *Verse Daily*.

"To Ease My Mind" appeared in *Poetry Daily*.

"The Nuns' Remains" was reprinted in *Pontoon Five: An Anthology of Washington State Poets*, Floating Bridge Press, 2001.

"No, you have the wrong number," appeared in *Poetry on Buses 1998*, published by 4Culture with support from the King County Department of Transportation.

Thanks to Farrar, Straus and Giroux for permission to reprint a line from Robert Lowell's poem "Epilogue," *Collected Poems*, 2003.

I am grateful to the following organizations whose generous funding supported the preparation of this book: Artist Trust for a 2002 GAP Award and a 2003 Literary Fellowship, The Seattle Office of Arts and Cultural Affairs for a 2004 CityArtist Award, and The National Endowment for the Arts for a 2005 Literary Fellowship.

Many thanks to Nine Poets, a.k.a. The Poor Man's MFA, past and present, for their critique and fellowship, especially Catherine Wing, Ron Starr, Kirsten McAteer, Rebecca Loudon, Martha Clarkson, Jared Leising, Beth Kruse, and Peter Pereira. Thanks to Carlos Martinez for our exchange. I am deeply grateful to Stephen Dunn, Peggy Shumaker, Hilda Raz, and the University of Nebraska Press. To my teachers Jim Deatherage, Michael Hickey, Albert Goldbarth, and especially Sharon Bryan, who nurtured this collection: love and thanks. Steve—you made this possible.

Famous

1 Minor Characters

The League of Minor Characters

The main character sits on his childhood bed
naming everything that's gone—ex-job, ex-wife,
ex-best friend—and finally apprehends

the breakdown we've felt coming since chapter five.
When his doctor calls with test results, most of us
decide to remain minor characters

like the quixotic neighbor growing
bonsai sequoias, or the waitress with thick
glasses and a passion for chess,

because the main character, in the thrall
of a relentless plot, can't help hurtling toward
the crumbling cliff edge. And who needs that?

Some inherit genes from generations
of minor players, some must learn to guard
those sunny Sundays with the paper

full of heroes in distant gunfire. And some of us
who've gotten smug over the years turn another page,
turn on the football game, until one day

the doorbell rings. We close our books,
adjust our eyes, and the protagonist
sweeps in insisting himself into our lives

with his entourage of lust and language,
sorrow, brio. Hero, anti-hero, it hardly matters
with the lights this bright. The music crests

and it's time to speak.

It's Not You, It's Me

Nature abhors a vacuum
but God loves a good vacuuming.

The garden was strewn with petals
and those whimsical helicopter seeds
so God created woman and watched
as Eve unwound the cord, plugged it
into the slot between good and evil
and tidied the footpaths
while all the animals sat there, dumb,
and when she was done

somebody got out the apple juice and spilled
somebody opened a box of crackers
somebody trimmed his nails without a thought
for collecting them in his palm

and after however many days of consecutive Eden
Eve said I gotta get outta here and she did
and the cord snaked after her.

The International House of Pancakes

Under that blue plastic fake chalet roof5
there are people eating waffles
at ten o'clock on a cloudless Monday morning.

Everyone with a destination
has eaten breakfast and gotten on with life,
so they must be uncertain tourists

bent over plates of butter and sweetness,
ducking a sky so bright and blank
it could point anywhere, mean anything.

I've got a reservation at the hospital next door
which I'm pretending is a Ramada,
that I'm just another jittery traveler

with overnight case and toothbrush.
I could pull in, add to this lump
in my stomach. It's a good place to go

if you're a stranger, alone, almost forty
and late to see the world. The menu unfolds
like a map and for a moment your trip

feels intentional. But if you look, the diners
are not travelers at all but castaways,
their islands shrinking with every forkful

until they drift out the door
on this brilliant day, no place else
they want to go, no place far enough away.

LOST COAT, PLS CALL

Even in Sporting Goods, even as my son
grinned at it in the three-way mirror,
that coat started disappearing,

slipping in and out of the material plane.
Even as I wrote his name
on the inside tag below *Men's Small*,

as if that would fend off loss, it started
to look missing. We try to be optimists here,
we send him out each morning in a coat

and he comes back with it sometimes.
Even after a Samaritan came upon it in a field,
read the name and tracked him down,

he didn't really own the coat, he'd only
borrowed it until he could return it
to the universe, the way at two he cast

his first hooded fleece from his stroller.
That one had drawstrings with wooden toggles
and I dreamed of it once, hanging

on a scarecrow. In my dreams I revisit
them all—the red Gore-Tex, the green slicker
with cargo pockets, the beige fleece

and the blue fleece and the rust jacket with
yellow sleeves. They hang on fence posts,
in magic closets extending into parallel worlds,

on air currents like sea gulls—coats soaring
on uplifts in the cold and rain as my son
lopes along below, in my arms one moment,

the next out the door, insufficiently warm.

The Nuns' Remains

On the eighth day of rain,
the nuns—
stacked in twos
in their Calvary graves—
washed down the hill
to our own back garden,
where each found
a bed of her own.
Mostly they favored
golden rays of early daffodils
or the pheasant eye narcissus
with its delicate crown.
But one chose
the tender white blossoms
of a freesia
which we brought inside.
It smelled like black pepper
and illumined the dark.

Map of the Marriage Bed

Some nights he wants directions
and she tells him which crossroads,
where to idle, where to drive fast and hard.

It's instinct, and the route into those mountains
wanders—on the back of an elephant,
on the lip of a milk jug, jangling, jangling.

Some nights only half-way there he pulls
into a motel hidden in a grove of Douglas firs
because they're lost—they're always lost,

but some nights on those unlit highways
it hits him hard—and he takes charge,
produces a key, a chair, a lamp, and the Puritans

who live inside them nod at the trim hospital
corners, the porcelain ewer and basin. They
take their places, grip and grimace in the dark.

And a few times one has hauled off
and clapped the other flat on the head,
hijacked their moving vehicle and driven overland

until the nettles and tumbleweeds put a stop
to this craziness. They crawl out the passenger
window, they weep, they say a little prayer

and cling to each other in the grass and dirt.
Once she found a knife in the field where they lay.
And once she found a ruby ring.

How to Read This Story
to Your Children

When you *woof* for the dog,
imagine him gray at the muzzle,
profound and gentle, but
with a taste for tasseled loafers.
The clock in the hall *tick tocks*
with an Eastern European accent;
the scissors *snip* crisply
as a nurse in starched cap.

The child in this story never ain'ts
or slams doors or speaks insincerely,
and he's suspiciously good natured.
You'll need to intimate with your pauses
the sticky striped candy hidden in his fist,
and in the spaces between words
those midnight walks
when he sneaks into a field
of sunflowers and stars.

When Father speaks,
put a slight yawn in his voice,
as though he's only just
wakened into his life,
the delicacy of his son's bones,
his wife's cotton dress,
the morning home free from
the mysteries of work. Where
have I been? he seems to ask
behind his newspaper.
How do I enter the story?

And the smiling mother,
who speaks of nothing
but blueberries and making jam—
let her voice have an edge to say
she hates the hot work of canning,
the too-small house.
The sweeter and more patient her words,
the more impatient she sounds,
hinting she might shout with dismay
if her child asks one more question,
or run out and cut off all her hair.

When you're narrating, be the voice
of kindness, your very best self,
but a little removed
as if watching from the top banister.
You read in warm blue tones suggesting
dog and boy, father and mother
retrace their steps
over countless readings,
that no matter how they never learn,
you forgive them everything.

Elisabeth Reads Poetry

Elisabeth is two and reads
a book of poetry off my shelf,
opens with *Yah yah sumpin to eat.*
I try to read my own book
but she sings *Dibbah dah ze Rosie.*
She's changed her clothes
six times today
from blue dress to swimsuit
to Tom's size 7 green jeans.
That was all before 10:00.
She's been naked ever since,
now reciting *ABDB's,*
while I read over her shoulder
to check for genius,
like my friend who found
her two-year-old breaking
the alphabet code,
reading real words
as if he'd climbed
into the high cupboards,
eating sugar and poison
willy nilly—a horrifying miracle.
But no. *Atsa batta sorry,*
Elisabeth intones
and tosses the book in favor
of a red crayon, then
on to her dolly's baby blanket,
folding it like soft origami.

I thumb her dropped book of poems.
I can't help it, she's a genius
of prolonged babyhood,
of its light, its wild uncoded rhythms,
playing late into the open afternoon.

Life and Art

The artist, nine, has only just discovered the vanishing point.
The two white lines painted on the bottom of the shoebox
converge, depicting a country road. Pipe-cleaner forest

borders both box sides, fading toward a crayon sunset.
Perspective is her first innovation. The second: point of view.
The observer looks down like god or giant upon this scene.

A matchbox car is driving toward its future. Not
just any matchbox, but the old box van she unearthed
in the backyard garden. And in the back seat, too dark to see,

an imagined brother and sister. They are leaving the city
for the very first time. *This is the moment they behold
the forest*—it inflames the artist's mind.

Though she's never seen a city, she lives in the forest
and knows which is more important. She knows
the tiny children can foresee their future:

a pretty house drawn in fine point just below the sunset,
which to a careful eye reveals its gables and chimney,
wishing well and picket fence.

And her third innovation: a peep hole,
an alternative view of the scene,
fitted with a lens swiped from Father's dark glasses.

It deepens the shadows, the distance, the highway lines
disappearing in a crayon blaze, that forest
she will spend her life and art trying to describe.

Passing for Mormon

is easy, as I dream my way through Utah
on I-15, bathed on a slick of sunscreen
in a blue reflecting motel pool.

My splashing children, comfortable
manner, that shy sly look
of recognition I perfectly deliver—

I know they know I am.
For a few days we live among them,
climb the red cliffs and hoodoos

by day, sleep in identical Best Westerns.
I walk down Main Street, point
to the golden angel Moroni, willingly

suggest that he is holy. Christ
it's hot. How did their persecuted
elders ever get the guts

to drop their bones here and chicken
scratch a living in their petticoats,
or sustain a fairy tale so long?

I cultivate the waitress's error,
order Pepsi with dinner. I'm pleased
to be clean cut, pleased to breaststroke

in a modestly attractive swimsuit. I try on
their particular cock-and-bull story
and hypothesize like a scientist

that a switch must get toggled in the brain
or a node just falls asleep, guess
at what greater sleight of hand

allows us to believe the unbelievable.
As if I didn't know.
As if I didn't know exactly.

No, you have the wrong number

though you sound open as a state on the plains, a tall man
strolling into town for directions and refreshment. I step out
from the dark behind the phone, offering a cool drink,
rangeland under my apron. I can hear your eyes
on the line grow wide, like the moment grows wide—
then the click, dead air, and a dust storm.

What I Learn Weeding

18

A dandelion root can grow two feet long.
You don't forget unearthing one—shocking
as a donkey in an old French postcard.

But mostly, love, we pull their heads off
to achieve our shallow vision of a garden.
The root cleaves to the darkness,

the same dark that sets our hips to rocking,
to burrowing into the other's body
or slapping it away. Briefly a stillness,

a long waiting to rise. Respiration. Sleep.
Until, without nurturing, a green shoot,
a thumb raked lightly across a thigh

and we succumb to this buried fury, this fever
to reseed. Oh, subterranean marriage
of root and soil! Oh, saw-blade leaf

and sunburst of maddened flower!

Everybody Wang Chung Tonight

Bemused. Fixed on a blowsy fuzz ball, or
a spider delicately crossing a Delaware of wall.
Recumbent in a tent of fashion magazines
and overdue, overlarge bills. Everybody now.

From your recliner. While a war unwinds
on TV. While the deck rots out from under.
Shake it baby. These evenings, thin as glass
and slipping just as slowly downhill.

They're what make you what you are.
Not those engraved occasions, white-tie audiences,
Everybody raise a toast, not the great seduction scene,
remarking on the perfect height of the desk,

but the way you spend your real life, succumbing
to the siren call of ice cream and original Star Trek.
The dead skin of a quiet evening spent talking to yourself
like this: what do I want? what can I have? etc.

Calling Up Ghosts

I can always find Dad frying bacon in the kitchen.
I take a stool while he pours orange juice and offers me
the Sunday paper. I read Richland's scores aloud
and ask him to explain "B.C." It's our way

of marking time until Mother wakes up. Maybe
because she died first, she's undependable about rising,
which makes us anxious, walking room to room
around the house, which is sold now,

Mother's Stickley and Spode, Dad's books parceled off.
Dad doesn't notice that everything is gone, only
that Mother feels nearby but missing.
He grabs my shoulders to give them a reassuring squeeze

when an ache almost bursts my throat, that cry of children
lost in department stores who know better
than to make a scene, yet it rises anyway, a squeak, a croak,
and there she is, lit up and comforting,

You know I'd never leave you! Oh dear, I was here all along.

A Middle Child is Born

His birth at dawn was easy by the standard
of the first one. The sky remained white all day,

or rather, that small chunk between office buildings
visible from her hospital window.

It was Friday, day of industry. She spied one tower over
a woman bent like a seamstress at her computer,

then down at this tiny red soul, his nose straight
out of a gangster movie. Her first son toddled in,

gave a round of hugs, opened brother gifts
and toddled out with Daddy. Nurses peppered

the afternoon. Around 2:00 she wept violently
for the ruined life of her radiant firstborn.

She caught a glimpse of a woman her age
gesturing boldly in a business meeting,

then three cleaning women making rounds
with their spray bottles and vacuums.

The day was long, like any spent lolling in pajamas
with a new companion short on talk

and a little standoffish. Attending
to a careful inventory of toes, swirls, delicate veins,

and crying. Grave with perfection
and all the ways she would let him down.

22   The office lights doused now. His navy eyes open.

The Physiology of Joy

In the bleakest centers of the body, researchers
have discovered tiny pockets of joy,
like the undersized bubbles that cling
to the corners of parched mouths.

We're trying to understand, the spokesman said.
He was staring into the camera. They might be
an immune system response to pain
or evidence that joy
in order to be released
must coalesce to a critical mass.
Then he leaned into our living room
to confide

that in his college anatomy class,
sometimes the bodies would sigh
at the end of a long dissection,
an unaccountable flutter under his hands.
Once he was last one out
of that blue gymnasium of a laboratory.
I don't know if it's proof, he said,

but when I switched off the lights
the transom windows glowed.

11 Minor Celebrities

Graphology

Your I's lie on their backs. They look like 2's.
You lead a double life. Your V's are spread,
about to fly away. Your O's threaten to tell on you.

Your Y is very large. Y is ruining your life.
I advise a smaller Y. Likewise your C is wide open
and your G's tongue is thrusted, cupped

as though to taste something it's long resisted.
Everywhere too much mouth. Capitalize your A's
to look like praying hands, soon.

Trim your tails, space your words
a safer distance apart. Some are mingled,
confused where they stop and start.

Keep m's small and low like fists.
Slope your R's like a crone hoeing the ground.
You leave footprints on the snowy page.

I can see where you're going. Turn around.

The Minor Celebrities

The restaurant critic in your city, perhaps,
with his predilection for chocolate and free wine.
Or the latest cleaned-up mayoral candidate.
The history teacher on parole for
the taped phone call with his student aide—
celebrity and flagrancy often hand in hand.
The girl who had it all in high school,
Broadway-bound but never made it out of town.
The lover in a major poet's poem,
draped naked at either end or slipping
in and out of the poem's surface like a dolphin,
slick with the words you want for your own.
Or the major poet himself, famous only
in small, uncelebrated circles and at home in bed.
The good Samaritan, especially
if something bad befalls him.
The news anchor who reports his fate
in careful, disappointed tones.
The woman working with your husband
whom you've never met. Anyone
the one you love loves.

Salute them now. For making the days go by,
one sliding into the next in succession.
For creating a backdrop. For stepping aside.

Words drift down on Virgil Suarez

while he takes dictation. Poems
sway above his desk, island girls
fishing for boyfriends.

In England, sheep with words
sheared into their fleeces
graze, revise their poems

by changing places.
On a sunburned plain in Chad, a girl
writes a couplet to persuade the rain

to fall. In Soeul, one neon word
flashes bright on a cold tenant's
window all night and Virgil Suarez

sees this frozen message
from his desk across the world,
glazes it across a sonnet's last line.

A Delhi woman bludgeons her father
with words. He bites his tongue.
The sheep spell out his answer and erase it.

Startled awake, I let the book slip from my hand.
My dead father's voice like a clapperless bell
swings above my head.

It starts raining in Chad.

Sarah Chang plays violin

and stamps her foot like a flamenco dancer.
White flames lick the hem of her Madame X dress
and the orchestra leans in, warming their hands

to her fire. The heat of her furious bow.
Her smoke. She's rubbed Tchaikovsky free
of his genie bottle. He is ready to grant any wish.

A man seated two rows down begins
to tic and twitch, his finely shaved neck
in a spasm of abandoned control. His wife

turns to him, concerned, wraps her arm
loosely about his shoulders. And you and I?
A man in rapt profile and his wife, a spigot

of weeping, streaming gratitude to this girl
whose playing reveals who I am—lover,
mother and daughter, afraid, alight, awake,

alone. Nothing, again, we'll ever talk about.
I grab your enormous hand and let her violin
sing what I can't say myself. As we drive home,

two cars cut and weave through the steady traffic.
Their tail lights careen. We gasp but they
cross untouched and bleed into the future.

You can't hear her anymore, I almost ask
as you touch and touch the brake.
And you switch on the radio.

Pantoum for Jane Goodall

The hunters dream of eating Jane Goodall for breakfast.
Jane dreams chimpanzees spring from her forehead.
Jane wakes and barely escapes into the forest
when the hunters' stomachs rumble like premature gunfire.

Jane dreams chimpanzees spring from her forehead.
The chimpanzees dream of sleeping with Jane Goodall.
When the hunters' stomachs rumble like premature gunfire
they fumble possession of Jane's tender morsels.

The chimpanzees dream of sleeping with Jane Goodall.
They sign their dreams to no one, confused by desire
and fumble possession of Jane's tender morsels.
Jane records their stillness and scratches her belly.

They sign their dreams to no one, confused by desire
and girly-show glitter beyond the familiar forest.
Jane records their stillness and scratches her belly.
The chimps bang their chests and swing toward the city.

Girly shows glitter beyond the familiar forest
where hunters dream of eating Jane Goodall for breakfast.
The chimps bang their chests and swing toward the city.
Jane bares her body and dances in the forest.

Edna St.Vincent Millay's Husband

In the garden, in his gardening togs,
he cuts back the grapes till noon,
then two drinks in the kitchen before
he writes his wife a letter which includes

his sad advances on a family friend,
a dutiful report of their coupling,
and a delicate probe into her state of mind
in Paris with her newest lover-protégé.

Later, in silk trousers, he pours a drink
by the pool, eats dinner on the patio
and tabulates her debts and royalties,
the escalating costs of her morphine,

winds the clock by their bed,
takes a toddy and assorted pills,
pens another letter proposing she return
before month's end and the frost

to see the garden before it dies.
Oh the beauty of his wretchedness.
She must have ached for it a little,
the stylish way he offered up his aching,

as she came back and let him care
for every need. Swaddled in gauze
or lordly in black and blue,
love is a fiend.

Built Like That

The alphabet makes love to me

while the tots are at school. I unlace

my straps, adorn my knots with jewels.

The dogs, poor dogs, how they howl

when the ravishing passes by, that slow

revolving cherry. O Monsoon,

must you cling, I'm already drenched

in juice? Tassels rain down, golden pods

and catkins. And the dark's obdurate wheel

rolls forward and back crushing plains of grass

into meal, plains of grass, a song

that will ruin me.

What I Saw

Memory jumbles which I noticed first—
the bicycle abandoned in the grass,
discarded clothes, or sounds of splashing
in the lake. She emerged from the weeds

still wet, toweling dry, and must have seen me
round the path, kicking through the leaves
and morning frost, my sympathetic shiver,
though she never met my eye. She turned

her back but didn't wait to peel away
her seal-black suit and what I saw
was ampleness and white, the beauty
of the world in late September.

Sometimes when I think of it I stare.
Sometimes she is me and I am her.

Conversation with a Sensualist

He plants *palm fronds* in a sentence
and lets them blow a warm trade wind
from his lips. She feels the heat,

tucks in every verb and smoothes
her sentences, folds them as neatly
as linen napkins, accordion-pleats them

for a touch of style. When he invokes
eroticism—a word she's never actually said
out loud—its syllables recline spread-eagled

on the chaise longue of his tongue.
His question marks all swirl and curve,
their currents play with her skirt.

She blanches her answers *sensible*,
but her blush is pronounced.
He hears it well enough and smiles.

Her defense devolves into dots and dashes
in her mouth, an oral SOS,
then even the S's say too much

and all that's left is *oh oh oh*

Dust

We move in clouds of our own dust,
invisible transmuting fields of lint, debris,
flaking skin and yes, dirt entrained from the earth

that follow us, billow when we stick our hands
in our pockets, stamp our feet or swing a bat
at a ball. We're no better than Pig Pen,

you and I, with an extra flourish—a geyser of dust
gushes from our pates like a Carmen Miranda
headdress, perhaps the detritus

of our mundane thoughts or—*dust to dust*—
little bits of our own deaths which mingle
when we kiss. See? The tops of our heads

really do shoot off—sparks that any good
electron microscope could spot, even
when it's rote, even when your hand as usual

goes there and I arch my back like this,
I'm making grocery lists and maybe
you're wishing I were someone else.

On those days that can feel desperate
as the end of the world, I remember the merging
of our dust and matter, which is cosmic, after all,

descended from comets. We burst
like fountains, we shimmer—with proper
magnification we'd astonish ourselves.

You see? Those old fireworks still there.

Lessons in Trigonometry

I learned my legs were two sides,
the rolling horizon of his back
the hypotenuse, and it moved

into place, from right to the difficult oblique.
I discovered my genius in the classroom
for sines and after-class tangents,

for triangulating the long waxed hall,
angle of the eye, measured walk
and platform turn, given one inscribed,

one circumscribed circle. For the fundamental
identities—his/how I broke down,
mine/not mine, woman/child.

By the final I could calculate the paths
of two planes flying in unsteady wind.
I applied what I'd learned of immutable law,

predicting their distance and wreckage.

Colonel Mustard Between Games

I find my bench in the conservatory,
nurse a scotch and this throbbing headache

and contemplate my id. I'd like to get my hands
on that wee revolver, the tiny gold wrench,

I can almost feel the knife between my fingertips.
When I'm idle I'm just a cartoon of a man,

a loser with a handlebar moustache.
I'm no smarter than Miss Scarlet in her

tawdry side-slit dress or Mr. Green,
the regrettable car salesman. These interludes

undo me. But roll the dice and everybody stares
when I enter a room—they write my name

on their detective pads. Motive, desire—
I've got it all in spades. But have I acted?

That's the hell and hardest part of this game—
the heart stays sealed, its capacities a mystery.

Sea Monster

We've gathered the experts to sound the loch
and map its deep bathymetry,

the child psychologists, the family therapists,
the counselors from "Camp Courageous Kids,"

some with their listening equipment, some with their
shaman prayers and sixth senses for the dark,

and some of us who just feel safer knowing
the size and shape of two daughters' grief.

We stand on shore to meet its filmy inner eye.
We wait to see it rise and blink. But the animal

sleeps. Therapy is quiet, the girls play soccer,
collect stuffed animals and get good grades.

Our measurements are all remote—
we note how hard we push and they push back,

how fast their faces close at their mother's name.
Once when somebody said "suicide"

we all rushed to see the surface break.
Nothing. How often have I wakened

and thought of her, their mother, whom I loved,
how she drove to a terrain as bleak as the moon,

loaded her backpack with rocks and jumped
to the bottom of a lake? I believe

in monsters. I believe in their cunning. She
taught me that they rise up when no one is looking.

I stand by with the divers, technicians,
their father watching out for any sign. This time

I'm going to be there to strike the monster down.

Shampoo

This is solace: a bowl of shredded wheat
softened perfectly in milk and today's paper

turned to the Lifestyle section.
The Russian sub is pinned front-page down

on the bottom of the Barents Sea. I'm dipping
into "The Dos and Don'ts of Shampoo,"

the distinction between lathering and cleansing,
a crown of suds in my imagined fingers

and just like that I'm lost in the silver
of my mother's hair, back in the hospital

where she sank into infirmity, her heart foundering
and all of us helpless, standing by.

I hadn't brushed her hair since I was a girl,
or ever fed her pared fruit with my hand.

A man with an ultrasound machine
pointed to the soundless blips

and in the shadows of that small screen
we saw her trapped inside her aging body.

The divers still hear taps. If I stop to think
I'll hear them too. One hundred eighteen men

in a vessel I imagine falling
like a pearl in a bottle of green shampoo.

Gil's Story

Gil tells you his story in the company truck
on your first job under his wing.
He cuts the engine and pulls

to the shoulder, which is alarming.
He's a big man who talks rough all day
to drillers, but you know he's kind—

everybody in the office says so. Gil's
a sweetheart, they say without elaboration.
He rolls to a stop and waits,

which prepares you, I think; it wipes
the fake smile off your face. He clears
his throat, then it streams like a steady well—

that lazy drive home from vacation,
his wife napping in the camper
before she and their daughter switch,

his careful introduction of the boy
who has drifted an entire lifetime
into their oncoming lane. It's beautiful

really, the way they crash into the boy's
car, how it parts the boy's curtain
of long blond hair and death anoints him

with a dot of blood on his forehead.
A single hubcap bounds like a tin deer
across the highway. Gil's frantic wife

pries the camper open to find their dead girl
whose eyes are closed as though
she's dozing through a horror movie.

Then silence. Gil turns expectantly to you.
As you sit speechless, he'll nod
at whatever sound or breath escapes you.

He starts the truck with a roar
and you're driving again to the field.
All afternoon he babies you with the pipes,

the pump, and the rig. And when you return,
the whole office comes out to greet you,
touching your shoulder, saying your name.

If We Could Live Here

The plane is full. I sit in 20B.
Your profile in 19E
shines like a crescent moon.

The plane starts to taxi.
We are split by an aisle, a soon-to-be
fracture in the fuselage.

You turn to your seatmate
and by your gestures I recognize
your story about packing.

I am the recorder
of our last five minutes alive,
of unlikely water landings

and the gush,
of surrender to the enemy.
Love is large and simple

in the limbic system
when the rest of me
is stunned by fear,

in the moment between dialing
and ringing, or when I wake
from an immaculate sleep.

If we could live here—
engines screaming,
full throttle toward heaven—

all the daily baggage
would fall away. Imagine
the size of my love then!

Broken open, cast to the air
like seed—

it would be mad love, my darling.

The Beauty of the Curve

The curtain lifts on Bryant Elementary School's
Spring Recorder Recital. Ninety third-graders
fumble with their instruments, take a breath

and blow. Their parents, braced, breathe too
as "Hot Crossed Buns" emerges, a little scattershot—
the Normal Distribution brought to life.

By "Go Tell Aunt Rhodie," the audience
is moved by their sheer pretty-goodness,
though one kid knocks her music to the floor

and another squeaks to demonstrate
the tail below two standard deviations
below the mean. The curve implies

that somewhere on stage another kid
just played a note so sweet he might shatter
Mrs. Wedermeyer's glasses. And if

there are a mother and father who think
that child is theirs, may they be forgiven,
even if the child shining in their eyes

is moving his fingers slightly out of rhythm,
even if he's never led the bell curve in his life.
In consecutive measures of almost unison

it's easy to believe these children are musicians.
Their parents do, so stirred by "Ode to Joy"
they rise to their feet with the final phrase,

clapping from the darkened auditorium
at once, as one, heroically, like the parents
they've meant to be.

Sotto Voce

Tonight blame Kiri Te Kanawa
infusing the kitchen with her aria,
blame the mixed bouquet of basil

and flayed tomatoes and onions
and one expansive high note blooming
like a rose in fast-frame.

Here in the audience,
even in middle age, a little voice sings
from the back of the auditorium

of my throat. Aren't all of us
waiting to be discovered?
Men and women enter the grand halls

of regional sales meetings
pressing nametags to dresses and ties.
I have been one of those

entering hopefully, conducting
delicate exchanges in hotel rooms.
I have called those pale disclosures

my life. Blame the cheap seats
we bought in the balcony.
We barely hear the little cogs

in our own hearts. Mozart, they say,
heard entire operas in a moment—
second violins, a glaze of harp,

heroic voices in the chorus all
clamoring to be realized
at once. My genius may be small,

but sometimes truth rolls right at me
like a hard head of cabbage
and I see myself that suddenly,

draining the pasta.

III Fame

Fireball

Fingernails tap on the back door glass.53
It's Madge, who has crossed America

with her bottle of Palmolive to find you.
You invite her in and the rest is scripted—

the manicure, the porcelain bowl
of green suds. She leans close to whisper

and you know next she'll say
you're soaking in dish soap . . .

when dread escapes its straightjacket
inside a steamer trunk at the bottom

of that tank within you.
The darkness behind your eyes lights up,

director, gaffers and best boys stop.
You blink and your house is exposed,

false front split down the middle
on a drafty gray soundstage.

Madge fidgets with her snappy line
but you're awash and unable

to sustain your role, there's only time
to withdraw your hands from the bowl,

towel your fingers off
and slip into your painted yard,

through the *trompe l'oeil* gate
to a concrete corridor and exit sign.

Outside, the sun burns in its sky like a fireball,
which is what it really is.

Preservation

Bobo awaits my third grade class
at the forgotten end of the museum. I explain
when they finish beating their chests

that Bobo was a famous gorilla I saw at the zoo
when I was seven, that here he looks false
because he's stuffed and mounted upright, like a man.

We take in his flared nostrils and hair, the virility
of his chocolate-colored chest. Everyone, even Dylan,
falls silent for a moment, long enough to remember

you left me four weeks ago yesterday,
a rubber band snap to my inner cranium
for the thousandth time today.

Bess and Tran point to photos of Bobo as a baby,
dressed in a nightgown, being fed a bottle. Bobo "smiling"
at his birthday party. Happier days. I think irrelevantly

of the milk expiring in my refrigerator,
how attached I am to the date on the carton,
the day before the world went sour.

Even milk observes the rites of decomposition,
the holy rites that Bobo was denied.
Is that so wrong? Roy Rogers

stuffed and mounted Trigger, his companion.
Wasn't that sweet testament, if sad and strange?
Bobo, do you understand the impulse?

I gaze into your fake glass eyes but you decline
to answer. I'm talking to myself, your look implies.
We both stand awkwardly with nothing to say.

The kids are restless. They're talking about ice cream
and the bus outside. He was real, I remind them
but they're running up the hall.

The last time I saw him, he was alive.

One Night

an abridged biography of Shirley Jackson

One night in the middle of another
drunken party—the usual parade
stepping over cats and trash,
the lampshade making rounds,
her husband holding court,
her children running wild—
one night in the middle of real life

she found Dylan Thomas. There,
in her dirty kitchen, looking for a glass.
Sometimes I picture

just their shoes on linoleum,
circles inside circles, their complicated
scuff marks splashed with liquor and food,
hilarity coming and going through
a wide-swinging door. They moved
to the back porch to kiss
and nobody knows what else. But I think

the moon floated in and out of a cloud,
she passed him a secret with her lips
and became famous, finally, to herself.

After was merely after. Her solace
writing stories, her stories throwing stones.
I think back to her kitchen, the cat
on the counter, his scratchy tweed jacket,
his lips on her throat.
I replay the evening beginning to end

and in this very manner—
I'm sure of it now—
she got through the rest of her life.

Natural History

When I die, lava will flow and preserve me whole
for 50,000 years. I'll be exhibited in a great museum,
next to the whale bones and amethyst geodes.

You'll be pinned with the butterflies,
handled with gloves, exquisitely fragile.

Isn't it funny they'll never connect us?
This rock woman with that paper man?
They were never in love.
She would have pounded him into dust.
He'd have been crushed by a woman like that.

The Sound of a Train

I first heard it in the mornings.
I'd scan the hibernating garden and sky,
sure there were no tracks nearby.

Then other hours, other trackless hillsides.
Once along the leaf-blown lakeshore I heard
a train's wail—the very breath of grief. I turned

and saw a flash like a stag in the trees
before the dark scene stilled. Then I knew.
My mother and father were aboard.

My parents ride through the living world
and watch for me. If I could find their tracks
I'd wait patiently, the way I used to

at boarding gates, with lop-eared flowers
from the garden, hungry for stories
of their holidays away. But the ghost train

leaves no tracks. It never stops. Its stations
are unknown to me. My parents can't disembark
or catch my eye or say how good it is

to be together again. Another whistle announces
they are near, side by side, gazing out
at the world. I listen to them passing by.

What travelers they are.

My father invented the calendar

six days after my mother died.
He sat in her kitchen with visions of boxes

that could contain the house, the wind-tossed
apricot blossoms, her phantom voice.

He lined up the boxes in rows of seven
and to each column he bestowed a name—

a queue of pretty, indistinguishable nurses,
the same brown needle of medicine each time.

By cocktail hour, he'd overwritten them
with haircuts, doctors, and accountants.

He called that day the first,
put a slash through the 1.

My Mother's Biographies

were stacked on the green leather hassock,
fat books sheathed in library plastic.

After dinner and the dishes, after studying
the news, front page to the obituaries,

she took up her books and read.
She was the last to bed. I'd wake at night

to hear her bath, the waterfall
from an extended arm or leg.

After school I'd sit in her chair
and insert myself into her reading—

fur stoles, hunting lodges in the lake country,
dark figures in uniforms, ancient touring cars,

women who flew planes, who farmed African plantations,
women who authored books under pseudonyms,

women who fell in love with men not their husbands,
women who fell in love with women,

women who drowned themselves, or took poison,
women locked up with hysteria and delusions.

I couldn't ask—what would I ask?
Mother stood at the sink, working.

Woman Reading

She licks her finger, little flick   63
of tongue and fingertip on furlough
to turn a page—

a motion that distracts her.
The thread of phrase   is broken
but for the word at turning—

vessel.
Vessel as in *ship* or *blood*?
She has to pause, all context lost

but blouse and skirt, this urge
to take them off
                    an ache

for something to contain it all.
Maybe *vessel*, maybe *"el"* alone,
bobbing on the tongue. Maybe

luscious, maybe just a finger to her lips
is all the afternoon
was asking for.

And lays aside her book.

Murder Mystery

You're fingering the gun in your pocket
like a detective thinking like a criminal and then

a breeze off the lake ruffles the page, you shift
in your chair and your muscles remind you

of yesterday's steep hike. Page 186 already.
Now you're thinking like somebody on vacation,

of the tinkle of ice cubes from the cabin,
of your daughter's sylph silhouette against a faceted lake

and then your hand is on the gun again and pulsing
with adrenaline, you imagine slipping in the window,

rifling through files, turning to face an opening door
the way yesterday—after hard hours of climbing—

you imagined being pushed over the cliff into that cloudless sky,
your fall more swanlike than any Acapulco diver.

Your mind has turned liquid, as changeable and elegant
as the swallows that appear at twilight, and now

a cold martini pressed to one sunburned cheek, kissed lips,
and now a distant rowboat like a slow shuttle of silk,

and now this idea you could step out of your life
unafraid, with no worldly need but to find who done it.

Reading Hamilton's
Biography of Robert Lowell

and embarking on the final chapter, you might stall—
wander your house in search of stray candy, or heat
some lunch and eat staring at Lowell's bewildered face
across the table, as I did, but you won't keep

Lowell's plane from landing in New York, you can't
prop his "Beethovenesque" head in your hands,
which have returned to turning pages, alas, quicker
than you intended. You move swiftly. You've pared away

Hamilton's interfering voice, you've finally fought off
Lowell's relentless mother—how easily his father
dropped away—Lizzie has forgiven him again, *again*,
and the lithium mostly pins his arms and ears back

which *streamlines* his last few hours, this last doomed
among all the doomed attempts at peace and,
like that plane now landed, like the taxi driving him
back to his second ex-wife, you accelerate until

he can't bear the speed any longer, he slumps in his seat
because you couldn't stop. Though how you wanted to!
Not to prolong his suffering, but to see what beauty
he could make of it as he trembled to caress the light.

Ending with a line from Lowell's "Epilogue"

Anaïs Nin on the Sales Table

You pick it up
a Tuesday-morning innocent
read a random page
and smooth as old whiskey
slide inside

A bell trills on the door
A girl in pigtails stares
from her mother's hem

and you go down again
Up and down the wind
burns your lips
and moths fly out
your unbuttoned mouth

A man brushes by and coughs
You check your watch
and clamp your satchel shut

A Persian cat wandering the aisles
stops to rub the folds
of your cuffs, licks
something sticky off his paws

Just one more taste
You put the diary down
A bearded man
looks up from Kant
and watches you stride out

Keys, knobs
and blush-pink sky
a rush of cars, crossroads
of a thousand thousand
tongues

Miss Marianne Moore
Takes a Tango Lesson

Every dancer in the studio
lines up to sweep Miss Moore
into the close cockpit
of arms and thrusting torso.

A shoulder tap, then
a girl's fingers bony as wings,
or a young man's trim-sheathed
thighs. This dance is mine.

Like a V of migrating swans,
they take their turns at lead with
one well-pressed grosgrain ribbon
fluttering in their beaks—

she's a prime number aloft!
The pebble singing
in David's pocket slingshot!
She rolls her Rat eyes

and geometries collide
like bits of colored glass,
bejewelling light and downbeats
as everybody laughs—

Oh Miss Moore,
be our partner again!
the dancers ask her tricorn hat
en masse.

To Ease My Mind

If I woke as Mary Todd Lincoln

and if Abraham Lincoln slept next to me
like an uprooted tree, his knobby fingers

unearthed, his face a burl,
grey as a Mathew Brady photograph,

and if my country were at war,

my own cousins killing my cousins,
and I'd been told to tear the country's

damask down, shred its opulence
to bandage the wounded but

I knew it was hopeless, hopeless,
there'd be no stopping the blood

of filthy, putrid common men until
every human left had lost a child, a leg, an arm

and if I'd already given everything,

if I'd given over my grieving husband—
not without kicking and screaming—

and the birds were silent
to mark the never-ending end,

then God forgive me, perhaps I too
would turn my mind to the pleasures

of kidskin gloves adorned with pearls,
embroidered daisies and chrysanthemum

stars, white on white filigree so fine
one might believe a fairy tatted them.

I might need box upon box upon box of them
to tell me who I am.

Two Dreams of Infinity

I'm waist deep in glass beads in the middle-
school gymnasium each distinct and hand-
blown the colors of fruit candy
I am calm and sift
methodically
for a mate to the
planet earth in my pocket
so I may adorn myself with earrings

and then my daughter screams I hear
her screaming I rise in the dark
shedding incalculable detail
beads still rolling
from my sleep
and climb two stairs at a time
to my terrified baby who reaches
from her crib across the immeasurable night

An Informal Visitation

In a summer beach Dutch-door boutique,
in the throes of zipping into expensive orange cotton capris
gaily printed with parasols,

while beyond a paisley curtain the voices
of customers on holiday exclaim over ankle jewelry, beach glass,
and turquoise beads, the singsong of flattery,

I am wishing idly for my mother's hips
that would suit these crazy pants that do nothing for me,
for a little of her pantsuit glamour,

when Mother—as if I've stuck my head out the curtain
and called her back to the living for a fashion opinion—
joins me, appraises me stripped of the dark colors of grief

and offers to buy the outfit for me,
her big ectoplasmic purse hooked on her arm and her face
beaming approval. I dress and buy instead

a bracelet set with typewriter keys,
stroll Main Street down to the beach where a thick white mist
clings to the shore and turns all the families at play

into gray-scale tableaus of families.
I feel at once like myself and like a beautiful smiling stranger
emerging and reemerging from a curtain of fog.

The New Language

There will be perhaps six words for *snow*,
more than we have but not so many as the Eskimo,
ten more for *leaves*, two dozen for *ocean*

and at least a hundred for *wonderful* including one
reserved for old men in shorts and black knee-hi stockings
crossing against the light,
a few strictly matrimonial, a few obscene—
all of them onomatopoeic, pleasing,

and we will dispense, finally, with *always*
because it has wounded us both in different ways,
and substitute *a dinosaur epoch*
or a cinematic word for *shot-through-with-rose-and-gold sunset*
or the word *desert*, which will remain unchanged

as will *forgiveness* which will still retreat when I beg
but someday overtake us as we walk along its edge
in a synesthetic wave, my love,
a sudden rush and we'll be wet

with what will suck us back to the living
ready to speak with new tongues.

Prayer Animals

Pray to the sloth, the naked pig,
the foul-mouthed chimpanzee.
Look in the mirror
and remember humility.

Pray to the bull for his cock.
Pray to the cock for his crow.
Pray to the crow and the black
cloud of his brothers scudding
across the winter sky.

Pray to the neighbor's dog
who finally learned to live on a chain.
Pray to the rat in the attic,
rummaging through our handwritten sins
and Christmas ornaments.

And pray to the pink flamingo
who migrated north to a snowdrift.
When you're that fabulously wrong
and lost and cold, pray to be exotic.
Pray to be shocking and irresistible.